The Royal Wedding
29th July 1981

Above left: The Queen's procession was the first to drive along the flag-bedecked, crowd-lined route from Buckingham Palace via The Mall, Strand, Fleet Street and Ludgate Hill to St Paul's. The Queen and Prince Philip are seen here arriving at the cathedral. Below left: Many people in the jubilant crowd had camped overnight to gain a good vantage point along the route. Princess Anne and Princess Margaret, accompanied by Captain Mark Phillips and Viscount Linley, showed their delight at the cheering throng. Above: The Queen was greeted by the Lord Mayor of London at the steps of St Paul's, before entering the cathedral to take her place.

Above: *The next procession to leave Buckingham Palace was that of the Prince of Wales, accompanied by Prince Andrew. He and Prince Edward acted as Prince Charles's supporters, Prince Andrew taking care of the wedding ring of Welsh gold.* Above right: *Very soon afterwards, Lady Diana Spencer set out from Clarence House in the Glass Coach, seated beside her father and escorted by mounted police. The first glimpse of the bride showed a fairytale vision of silk tulle and lace.* Below right: *On her arrival at the cathedral, her dress of ivory silk taffeta was revealed in its full splendour. Lady Diana waited a moment to allow two of her bridesmaids to arrange her magnificent 25-foot-long train, before entering, on the arm of Earl Spencer, to a fanfare of trumpets.*

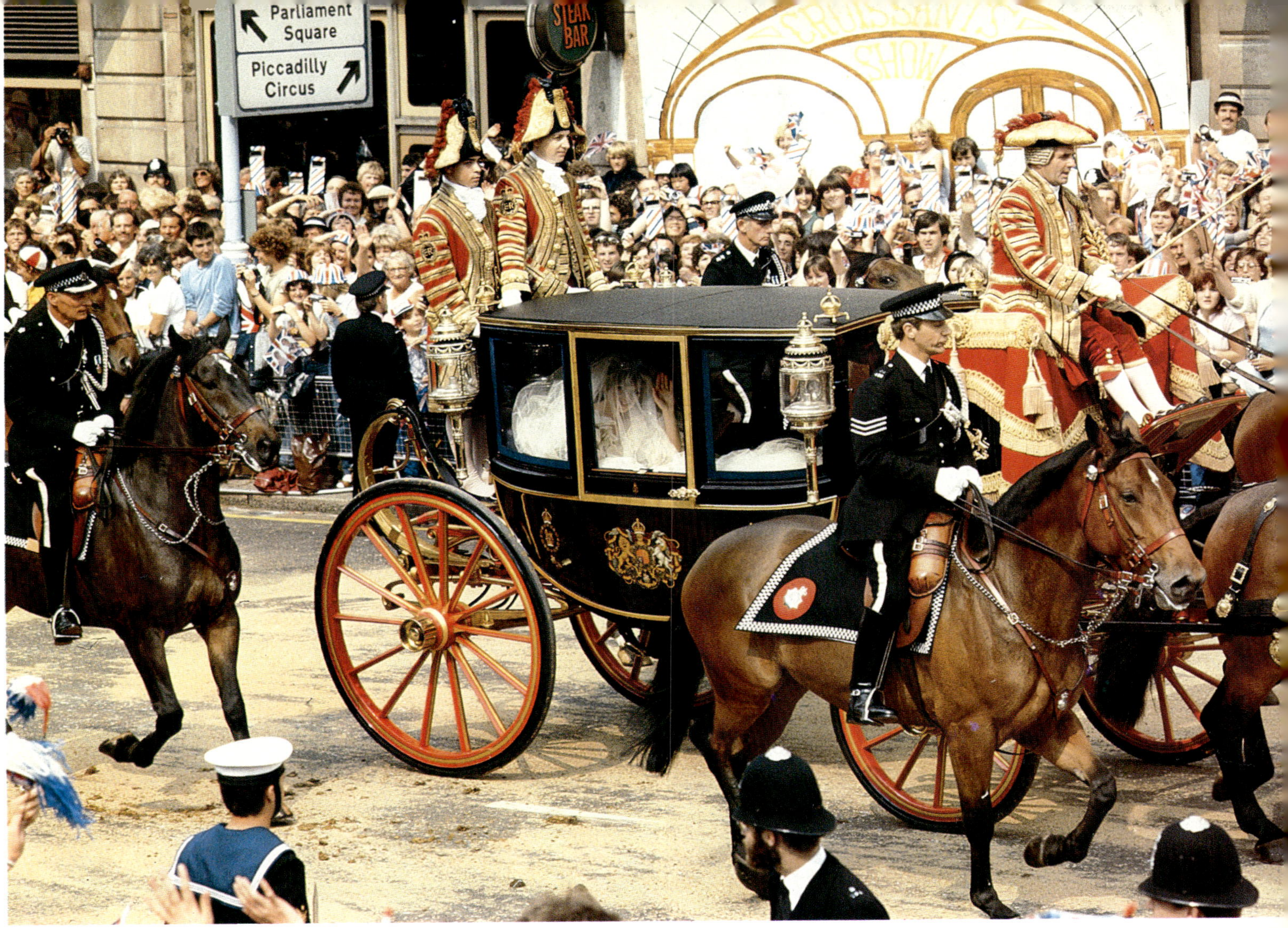
Parliament
Square
Piccadilly
Circus

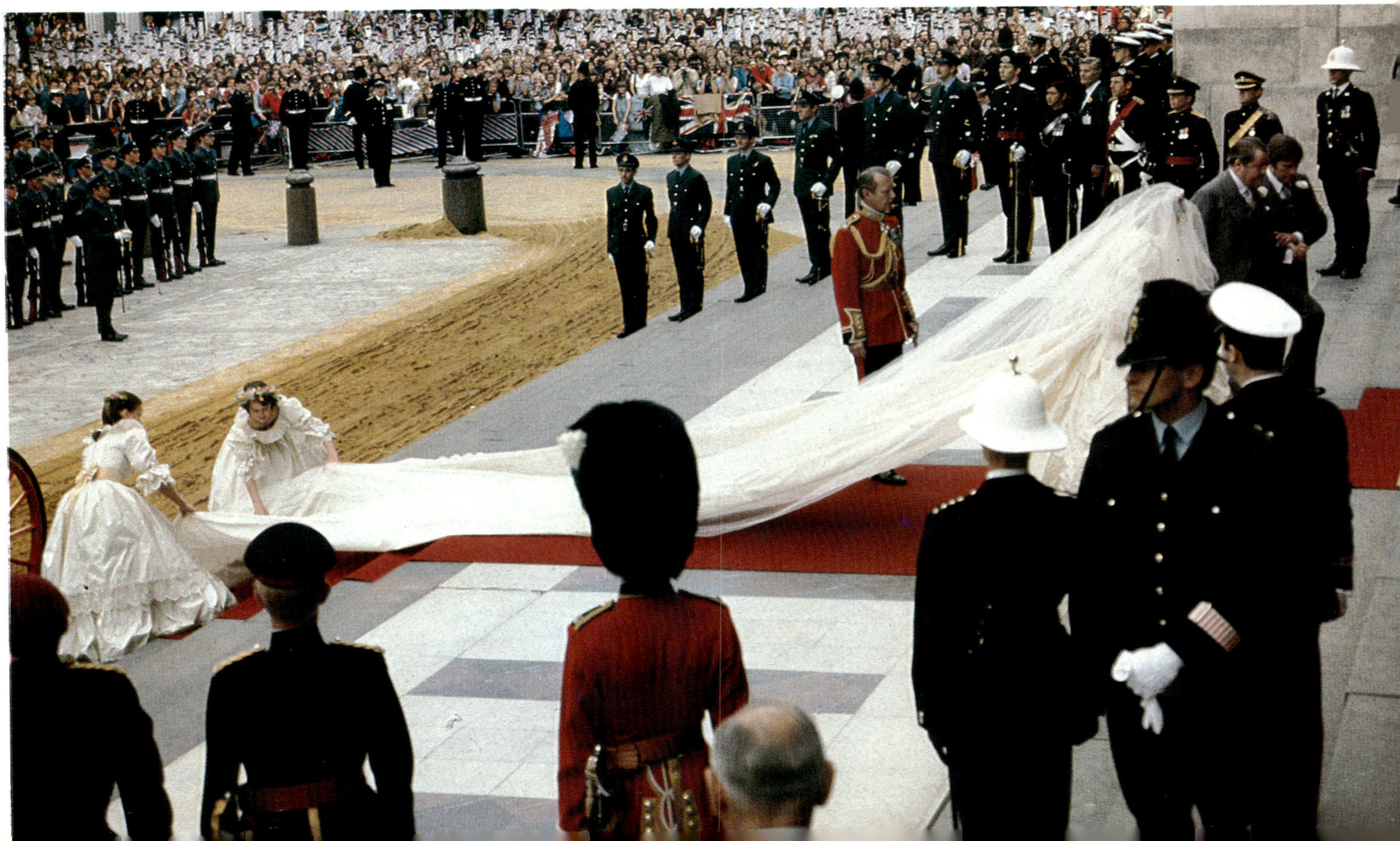

Left: *Lady Diana made her way from the West Door along the Nave as the organ and orchestra played the joyful Trumpet Voluntary by Jeremiah Clarke. She was escorted by her bridesmaids – Clementine Hambro, Catherine Cameron, Sarah Jane Gaselee, India Hicks and Lady Sarah Armstrong-Jones, enchanting in flounced silk dresses with flower circlets on their heads; and her pages – Lord Nicholas Windsor and Edward van Cutsem, in Victorian naval-cadet uniform.* Right: *Beneath the soaring dome of St Paul's Lady Diana was joined by Prince Charles, and together they went forward to stand before the Dean of St Paul's who began the service. The Archbishop of Canterbury performed the marriage ceremony. The service was solemn and deeply moving, yet also exultant in its emphasis on Christian marriage being 'the place where the adventure really starts'. The choir, organ and orchestra provided a musical setting of fitting splendour, including an anthem especially written for the occasion by William Mathias.* Below right: *After the signing of the Register, the Prince and Princess of Wales returned to the Choir to be greeted by a fanfare, followed by Elgar's Pomp and Circumstance March No. 4 as they proceeded down the Nave.*

Right: *The Prince and his bride were followed down the Nave by members of the Royal Family and the bride's family.* Below: *At the door of the cathedral, the Prince and Princess of Wales were greeted by a resounding cheer of welcome from the crowds. They stood for a moment to acknowledge the greeting* (frontispiece) *before moving down to an open carriage which took them back through the hundreds of thousands of spectators to the palace.*

Above: *As they drove, their happiness was overwhelmingly apparent. The carriage, embellished with a lucky white horseshoe, travelled at a spanking pace, postillions in bright livery controlling the horses.*

Top left: *Her Majesty the Queen returned to the palace with Earl Spencer, followed* (middle left) *by Prince Philip and The Honourable Mrs Shand Kydd, mother of the bride.* Left: *On arrival at Buckingham Palace, the Prince and Princess were greeted by children of members of the Royal Household, assembled in the courtyard, before alighting under the handsome pillared colonnade.* Top: *The bride and groom, members of both families and the bridesmaids and pages made the traditional appearance on the palace balcony shortly after their arrival. The multitude of people thronging around the statue of Queen Victoria and extending back up The Mall as far as the eye could see chanted first for Prince Charles and his bride, then for the Queen and the Queen Mother, who appeared and reappeared to wave to the crowd.* Above: *Prince Charles kisses his bride, much to the crowd's delight.*

After their appearances on the balcony, the Royal couple posed for formal photographs with family and friends before the Wedding Breakfast: Below, back row, *Captain Mark Phillips, Prince Andrew, Viscount Linley, the Duke of Edinburgh, Prince Edward, the Princess and Prince of Wales, Ruth Lady Fermoy, Lady Jane Fellowes, Viscount Althorp, Mr Robert Fellowes;* centre row, *Princess Anne, Princess Margaret, Queen Elizabeth the Queen Mother, the Queen, India Hicks, Lady Sarah Armstrong-Jones, Mrs Shand Kydd, Lord Spencer, Lady Sarah McCorquodale, Mr Neil McCorquodale;* front row, *Edward van Cutsem, Clementine Hambro, Catherine Cameron, Sarah Jane Gaselee, Lord Nicholas Windsor.* Left: *The Prince and Princess of Wales, glowing with love for each other.* Right: *Princess Diana, as beautiful and charming a bride as any Prince could wish for.*

Above: *The Prince and Princess of Wales travelled to Waterloo Station, to board the train for the start of their honeymoon, in an open carriage festooned with silver and blue balloons.* Left: *On the back of the carriage was pinned a handwritten notice proclaiming what few needed to be told!* Above right: *Princess Diana wore an attractive peach tinted dress and matching bolero.* Far right: *Broadlands, Romsey, Hampshire, the home of the late Earl Mountbatten; the Prince and Princess of Wales chose to spend the first part of their honeymoon in the tranquillity and seclusion of this beautiful estate. The handsome eighteenth-century house is set in fine gardens and parkland remodelled by 'Capability' Brown. The Queen and Prince Philip also came to Broadlands for their honeymoon, in 1947.* Below right: *Prince Charles and his bride then flew out to join the Royal yacht* Britannia *for a cruise in the Mediterranean.*

St Paul's Cathedral

The decision that the Royal Wedding should be in St Paul's was a departure from the recent tradition that such events should take place in Westminster Abbey. But Sir Christopher Wren's masterpiece, its dome rising high over the City of London, is a fittingly splendid setting for an occasion important to both Church and State.

The Cathedral was begun in 1673 as the replacement for Old St Paul's, destroyed in the Great Fire of 1666. Wren chose a combination of classical exterior with richly embellished Gothic interior. The Quire has fine wood-carving by the master of this craft, Grinling Gibbons, one of the many superb craftsmen Wren employed. The Dome, famous for the 'Whispering Gallery' running round its under side, is decorated with paintings showing the life of St Paul.

Above: *St Paul's Cathedral from the south-east;* above right, *the West front;* right, *the Nave, looking towards the High Altar.*

The Young Prince

Prince Charles Philip Arthur George was born at 9.14 p.m. on 14 November 1948, at Buckingham Palace. The crowd which had been waiting all day outside the Palace railings was told the news by a footman within a few minutes of the birth, and immediately began to cheer wildly. The following day saw gun salutes, peals of bells and flags flying as celebrations continued. His christening by the Archbishop of Canterbury took place a month later in the Music Room at the Palace. In the nursery at Clarence House, Helen Lightbody and Mabel Anderson cared for the young Prince, while Princess Elizabeth deputised increasingly for her father, now very ill. At the age of twenty-one months, the Prince gained a sister, and soon developed a 'most watchful and protective interest' in Princess Anne. They played happily together, enjoying games with their parents whenever busy schedules allowed, and going for walks in Richmond Park or on Hampstead Heath. On the death of George VI in 1952, Queen Elizabeth

Left: *Prince Charles at Clarence House in 1951.* Below left: *Arriving with his mother at the Guards Polo Grounds, Smith's Lawn, Windsor. In attendance was Viscount Althorp* (right), *the Queen's Equerry – his future father-in-law.* Below: *Visiting Smith's Lawn to watch his father play polo.*

succeeded to the throne. Charles attended part of the Coronation in 1953, watching the proceedings with interest; the Queen Mother was a reassuring presence beside him.

At five years old, he began lessons with Miss Catherine Peebles – 'Mispy' – then at seven became the first heir to the throne ever to attend an ordinary school, Hill House in Knightsbridge. The experiment was a success, and a decision followed to send him on to his father's old prep school, Cheam. After initial shyness and some holding back by his schoolmates, he settled down to a fairly happy four years, showing

Left: *sailing on* Bloodhound *at Fort William, Scotland.* Top and above: *Prince Charles at Badminton Horse Trials with Princess Anne and the Queen, in 1960.*

enthusiasm especially for geography, art, history and acting. While he was at the school, his mother announced her decision to make him, at the age of nine, Prince of Wales.

Charles moved from Cheam to Gordonstoun, in Scotland, again following in his father's footsteps. Here he learned to accept and make the best of conditions which at first appeared a little harsh. Just before taking his A levels, he spent two terms in Australia, at Timbertop, the bush outpost of Geelong Grammar School, and thoroughly enjoyed the experience.

Prince Charles became the first heir to the throne to read for a degree when he entered Trinity College, Cambridge, in October 1967, to study archaeology and anthropology, and then history.

In 1968 and 1969, while his studies continued, efforts were made to accustom Charles further to the formal world of pomp and ceremony he was about to enter, after the

Left: *The Prince as 'Reg Sprott, Singing Dustman' in a Cambridge revue in 1969.* Bottom left: *Prince Charles at Gordonstoun.* Below: *Prince Charles visited Whitehall in 1969, during a 'whistle-stop tour' of Government and industry.*

Top: *leaving Buckingham Palace as Colonel of the Welsh Guards for Trooping the Colour ceremony in 1978;* bottom left, *leaving St Paul's Cathedral after a service for the Order of the Bath;* bottom right, *inspecting Welsh Guards at Swansea in 1969.*

Above: with the Queen Mother in the robes of the Order of the Thistle; *right, leaving Caernarvon Castle in July 1969, after his Investiture as Prince of Wales.*

relatively sheltered life of school and college. In June 1968, Prince Charles was formally invested as a Knight of the Garter, in Windsor Castle. In his second year at Cambridge he found time to take part in the activities of the drama club. Later that year, he spent eight weeks at the University College of Wales, Aberystwyth, studying Welsh in preparation for his investiture as Prince of Wales. This took place at Caernarvon Castle on 1 July 1969. He swore an oath of fealty to the Queen and was presented by her to the Welsh people. The following February, he was formally introduced into the House of Lords. Despite these interruptions, at the end of his three years of study at Cambridge, Prince Charles gained a creditable Honours degree.

Service Life

Like many before him, Charles has used the armed services to teach him skills that are both fun and useful. He had learned to fly in 1968 while at Cambridge, but took an advanced flying course three years later at the RAF College, Cranwell. He also made his first parachute jump at this time. The Prince's career then changed direction – he entered the Royal Naval College, Dartmouth, in September 1971. After courses in navigation, seamanship and engineering, he joined his first ship, H.M.S. *Norfolk*, a guided weapons destroyer. His time spent in the Navy was enjoyable for the Prince and had its rewards for the crews he served with, for inevitably they were fêted at each port of call. He next served on a frigate, H.M.S. *Minerva*, where he was promoted to lieutenant before joining another similar ship, H.M.S. *Jupiter*, in 1974. At the end of that year Prince Charles trained as a helicopter pilot at Yeovilton, excelling in this demanding skill. In February 1976 the Prince of Wales gained his own command, a minehunter named H.M.S. *Bronington*. Initially it was planned that he should remain in the Navy for a further eighteen months, but he reluctantly gave up this career in December 1976 to undertake important Royal duties.

Above left, *as Colonel of the Parachute Regiment, at Aldershot;* left, *the pilot Prince;* below, *aboard* Ark Royal.

Relaxation

It is remarkable that in a life so crowded with public engagements, Prince Charles has found time to pursue so many interests of his own; many of them are sporting ones.

Even before he went to prep school, his aptitude for sport was encouraged. He was taught to swim well and to make good use of a gymnasium. At school the Prince took to all the dangerous outdoor pursuits – he enjoyed sailing (though his first outing with his father at Cowes was torture: he was horribly seasick), climbing, skiing and other physically demanding sports.

As Charles has grown older, his love of equestrianism has become his dominant sporting interest, to the delight of his parents, who share this enthusiasm. Prince Philip's skill at polo was certainly passed on to his son: in 1967 he began to play in his father's team. Later he was Captain of the Young England team and the Prince's polo gear is an essential part of the baggage for most overseas tours.

Just as Prince Philip fostered his son's love of horses, so his grandmother drew him to another sport, fishing. The Queen Mother was, when Prince Charles was growing up, the undisputed family

Top: *Prince Charles in disguise as 'Uncle Harry', when skiing at Klosters, Switzerland (he was playing a joke on press cameramen)*; above right, *relaxing at Balmoral on his 30th birthday*; right, *the Royal Family at Sandringham, Norfolk, in 1977.*

champion at fly-fishing. Since Charles spent much time in her company when his parents were away performing official duties, it was natural that she should teach her grandson the finer points of the art. His prowess brings rich rewards from the Dee on the Balmoral estate, and on trips abroad he has been known to make early-morning fishing excursions, the catch being eaten at breakfast. Shooting is another sport that can bring rewards for the table and here, too, Charles excels, with both rifle and shotgun.

One would think that this long catalogue of sporting interests would be enough for any man of action, yet many more could be added. Prince Charles enjoys a few days on the ski

Right: *with his great-uncle, Earl Mountbatten, at Cowdray Park in 1979;* below right, *talking to children in the Duchy of Cornwall;* below, *relaxing after a game of polo at Cirencester;* bottom, *learning how to manoeuvre a coracle, at Abergavenny.*

slopes each year, and in this activity his recklessness is said to make up for lack of experience. However, in this sport some luck as well as skill is needed to avoid the ever-persistent efforts of continental press photographers. Similarly, in any new sport he tries, for example surfing, there are always newsmen on hand to tell of a beginner's misfortunes. It is to Prince Charles's credit that he seldom 'loses his cool' in such circumstances.

Right: intense concentration shows on the Prince's face as he enjoys windsurfing at Cowes; far right, *learning the skills of polo from Prince Philip in 1965;* above, *with Uffa Fox on* Cowslip *during Cowes Regatta.*

Foreign Travel

Prince Charles's official travels abroad began in 1967, when at the age of nineteen he represented the Queen at the funeral of Prime Minister Harold Holt in Australia. He has now travelled to most parts of the globe, visiting mainly Commonwealth countries or those with strong commercial or historical links with Britain. Several engagements are crowded into each day; the demands of meticulous protocol mean that arrangements for a Royal Tour begin a year ahead of the visit. The seemingly endless introductions to briefly glimpsed officials and the constant interest expected to be shown by the Royal visitor would be an intolerable burden to most of us. But the Prince performs his duties with a polish which, however, never lacks charm or humour. He remains anxious to promote British trade and regards this as a vital part of his job.

Right, top: *with Prince Andrew in Canada, in 1977;* middle, *sun-tanned, relaxed and smiling, during a trek in the Himalayas in December, 1980;* bottom, *while visiting India in 1980, the Prince was bedecked with welcoming garlands.* Below: *in Calcutta, Prince Charles had a meeting with Mother Teresa.*

Budding Romance

After leaving the Services in 1976, Prince Charles's many activities included work with a number of charitable organisations. Two of these were instigated by the Prince himself: the Prince's Trust, and the Prince of Wales' Committee for Wales. But his continuing bachelorhood became increasingly the concern of the media. He had once declared thirty to be 'about the right age for a chap like me to get married'. As that thirtieth birthday passed, speculation as to the identity of a future bride intensified. A close friend of the Prince at this time was Lady Sarah Spencer. The Spencer family are distant cousins of

Above: *Earl Spencer distributes mincepies to members of the Pytchley Hunt outside Althorp.* Right: top, *Prince Charles with Lady Sarah Spencer;* middle, *Althorp Hall, the Northamptonshire home of the Spencer family;* bottom, *Highgrove House, near Tetbury, Gloucestershire, the country home of the Prince and Princess of Wales.*

the Royal family. Earl Spencer was an Equerry to King George VI and had a home – Park House – on the Royal estate at Sandringham before inheriting the ancestral Spencer seat, Althorp Hall. Through Lady Sarah, Prince Charles came to know her younger sister, Lady Diana. Educated at West Heath School and at a Swiss finishing school, Lady Diana had become a part-time kindergarten teacher in London. When it became known that she was a friend of Prince Charles, she was photographed and followed, but tried to continue her normal life.

Above: the Princess of Wales loves children, and enjoyed her job as a kindergarten teacher. Left and far left: her handling of the Press, before the engagement was announced, won her much respect and she rarely showed the pressure she was under.

Royal Engagement

The first hint of a serious romance came in July 1980, when Lady Diana was invited aboard the Royal yacht *Britannia* at Cowes by Prince Philip. The following month she received an invitation to the Queen Mother's birthday celebrations. Her subsequent visit to Balmoral, this time at the request of Prince Charles himself, enabled them to discover mutual interests and a love for each other in the open, yet private, surroundings both appreciate. The official announcement of an engagement came on 24 February 1981.

After the announcement, Lady Diana moved to Clarence House, home of the Queen Mother, and began to attend functions with Prince Charles. At the end of March, Prince Charles made a five-week tour of New Zealand, Australia, Venezuela and the United States of America.

Above left: *Prince Charles and Lady Diana Spencer on the day their engagement was announced;* above right, *the Prince and Princess of Wales share a liking for country relaxation – they enjoyed the peace and quiet of Balmoral during their engagement;* right, *Lady Diana talks to Princess Grace of Monaco during the first official event to which she accompanied Prince Charles.*

Following his return, the couple paid visits to many parts of the country, including one to Broadlands, the family home of the late Earl Mountbatten of Burma, where Lady Diana planted a commemorative tree, and another to Tetbury, the Gloucestershire town closest to

Above: *Her Majesty the Queen with Prince Charles and Lady Diana Spencer after the Privy Council meeting at Buckingham Palace on 27 March 1981.*

Highgrove House, their future country home.

Despite the many official events, Prince Charles also found time to take part in National Hunt racing and steeplechasing, with Lady Diana in the crowd to cheer him on.

Lady Diana's beauty, lack of affectation, commonsense and natural charm rapidly won her a place in the hearts of the British people, as the Prince and future Princess of Wales' love and support for each other showed clearly the happiness they can expect in marriage.

Above: *Princess Margaret and Lady Diana at Sandown Park with Prince Charles, who was taking part in the race meeting.* Right, top: *at Broadlands, Romsey, Hampshire;* middle, *at Tetbury;* bottom, *attending Royal Ascot.*

Photographic Contributors: Tim Graham; Keystone Press Agency Ltd; Patrick Lichfield; Popperfoto; Press Association; Rex Features; John Scott.